WILDFLOWERS OF ZION NATIONAL PARK

By Dr. Stanley L. Welsh

PLANT TAXONOMIST

BRIGHAM YOUNG UNIVERSITY

ZION NATURAL HISTORY ASSOCIATION

SPRINGDALE, UTAH

D0197025

ACKNOWLEDGMENTS

I wish to acknowledge all those whose photographs appear in this book. Many thanks to Steve and Nancy Clark, Larry Higgins, Larry Hays, Margaret Malm, Vic Jackson, W.J. Harding, John Stevens, and Sue Staebler.

I also want to acknowledge the contributions of Larry Hays, whose efforts helped assist the book to completion. He wrote the index and extracted the common names from the text. The coordination he provided with the Zion Natural History Association was invaluable.

Finally, the long walks taken to Northgate Peaks with Steve Clark and Larry Hays contributed greatly to my writing of this book. A special thanks to all who made my time in Zion so enjoyable.

— *Stanley L. Welsh*

PHOTO CREDITS

Steve & Nancy Clark, *33, 44, 57, 65, 119*
Larry Hays, *10, 16, 29, 37, 39, 98*
W.J. Harding, *75*
Larry Higgins, *32, 53*
Victor L. Jackson, *19, 101*
Margaret Malm, *13, 18, 21, 26, 28, 35, 45, 46, 50, 52, 54, 56, 61, 66, 76, 77, 79, 82, 84, 85, 87, 90, 92, 93, 96, 97, 99, 100, 104, 105, 107, 108, 115, 122, 126*
Sue Staebler, *125*
John Stevens, *Cover*
Stanley L. Welsh, *9, 11, 12, 14, 15, 17, 20, 22, 23, 24, 25, 27, 30, 31, 34, 36, 38, 40, 41, 42, 43, 47, 48, 49, 51, 55, 58, 59, 60, 62, 63, 64, 67, 68, 69, 70, 71, 72, 73, 74, 78, 80, 81, 83, 86, 88, 89, 91, 94, 95, 102, 103, 106, 109, 110, 111, 112, 113, 114, 116, 117, 118, 120, 121, 123, 124, 127, 128*

Text by Stanley L. Welsh
Project Coordination by Jamie Gentry
Technical Advice by Larry Hays
Design by Lee Riddell, Riddell Advertising & Design
Type set in Architect Bold and Baskerville
Lithography by Paragon Press
ISBN 0-915630-27-3

This book is dedicated to the memory of

Park Ranger and Naturalist

John P. Ethridge, 1950-1990.

John spent much of the last twelve years

of his life working in Zion National Park,

protecting, exploring, and interpreting it

to visitors. He knew Zion as few have.

The reverence, curiosity, and sense of adventure

which John brought to his life in Zion

set a standard for us all.

ZION NATIONAL PARK is situated near the western margin of the Colorado Plateau, where its waters drain into the Mojave desert, via the Virgin River. The Great Basin is immediately adjacent to the northwest of the Kolob portion of the Park. The Park's low elevation in Coal Pits Wash is at about 3800 feet (1150 meters); the high elevation on the summit of Horse Ranch Mountain is at 8926 feet (2720 meters). The total elevational range is thus over 5000 feet (1575 meters). Plants have entered the Park region from the Colorado Plateau, Mojave desert, and Great Basin. Other species represent extensions along the mountains of western North America southward from the boreal forests. Additionally there are a number of plants known from nowhere else; they originated in or near Zion Canyon and are known as endemics. Approximately 900 different kinds of plants (herbs, shrubs, and trees) are known from within Zion National Park. This book covers some 120 of the common ones and hints at many more. Some of the common species do not have showy flowers, but they are included here because they are so common. A few (the ferns and conifers) have no flowers at all. They are treated because visitors will see them along the trails in Zion.

Plant communities in Zion range from low elevation warm desert shrub up to ponderosa pine and fir. The very lowest parts of the Park are dry in most seasons and very hot in summer. The dry hot lands support desert plants such as blackbrush and saltbush. Whipple cholla, a much branched shrubby cactus, grows in the desert shrub communities. Fremont cottonwood, velvet ash, and other water-loving trees and shrubs grow along the rivers and streams and around seeps and springs. The trees are often festooned with canyon grape. Most of Zion Canyon's lower slopes and benchlands above the river are overgrown by the pinyon-juniper woodland, very common in the southwest, locally called "pygmy forest," and here consisting mainly of Utah juniper and singleleaf pinyon pine. Other plants in this community are Utah serviceberry, skunkbush, roundleaf buffaloberry, singleleaf ash, Mexican manzanita, Utah yucca, turbinella liveoak, and Gambel oak. Cacti, including the berry and plains pricklypears, grow in openings in the pinyon-juniper community.

Wet sandstone walls support peculiar plant assemblages called hanging gardens. These in Zion are often of the Windowblind type, with a flat face wall and an arch of stone at the top. The gardens support maidenhair fern, Zion shootingstar, Cardinal monkeyflower, yellow and red and yellow columbine, Zion daisy, and other water-loving plants.

Plateau summits and upper canyon slopes are clothed with ponderosa pine. The trees occur as slickrock and crevice plants growing with Gambel oak, mountain mahogany, bigtooth maple, rockplant, and numerous other species. Many moisture and shade loving plants grow in moist glades of the forests mantling the very highest plateaus. Green leaf manzanita is a main component of the ponderosa pine forests on the plateau summits, sometimes forming thickets of great size.

Discussions and photographs are arranged for ease of use. Plant species are grouped by flower color except for those plants that lack flowers or for those with inconspicuous flowers. These latter categories are included as a group at the end of those with showy flowers. The groups with conspicuous flowers are white or whitish, yellow to orange, pink to red or red violet, and blue to blue violet. Flowers vary in color within a given species; white flowered phases of practically all plant species are known, and flower color should not be thought of as infallible in species identification. However, the color arrangement represents the typical condition in Zion.

ON TERMINOLOGY

Botanical terms have been avoided except where their use leads to clarity of statement. Many botanical terms are used in the common language of a great many people. It is not unusual for people to think of something used in seasonings when the word herb is used, but to a botanist it simply means a plant that is not woody. A shrub, on the other hand, is woody, at least the main stems are mostly so, and it generally has a number of stems. Trees typically are larger than shrubs and generally have a single stem or trunk. It is obvious that trees and shrubs are perennial; that is, they live for more than two years. Herbs can be either annual (live one year), biennial (live two years), or perennial. Winter annuals germinate in the autumn of one year and flower, produce seed, and die in the spring of the year following.

Plants are classified into species (including subspecies and/or varieties), genera (singular genus), and families. Specific, subspecific, and varietal names are followed by the names of the botanists who described or renovated the names of the plants. They are included here to provide complete citations for those who might need them.

Common names vary from place to place for species with broad distributions. Some of Zion's plants have been introduced from Europe, where the plants have common names in several languages. We have attempted to provide the most usually applied common names of the region including Zion National Park.

ON POLLINATION

The beauty of the floral display is pleasing to human senses. Some of the plants are aromatic, causing us to pause when the sweet scent reaches us on gentle breezes. Both the floral display and the aroma are advertisements of the plants, kind of help wanted signs. A further attractant is nectar produced by glands at the base of petals in most flowers. The help wanted in most instances is that of insects and hummingbirds, which visit flowers because they are showy, aromatic, and have nectar and pollen as rewards. While at the flower, they transfer pollen from the anthers of the stamens to the stigma of the ovary. Such successful transfer of pollen is called pollination. The pollen grains, each in reality a tiny plant, grow downward into the ovary of the pistil to the ovules where fertilization takes place. The fertilized ovules develop into seeds and the ovary matures into fruit.

Red flowers are pollinated by hummingbirds, which visit flowers of other colors too; bees and other insects respond better to colors other than red and to aromas. Bees are able to see colors not apparent to the human eye, and when flowers are photographed using special film sensitive to those infrared hues, they appear strikingly different than what we think of as traditional flower colors. For example, some flowers we think of as brightly colored, yellow, pink, or blue might appear black to visiting insects. Bumblebees and beeflies visit massed flowers and those with broad tubular flowers, which can accommodate their thick bodies. Moths pollinate plants of the evening primrose, potato, and other families, whose flowers open in the evening and close the following morning. Such moths are said to be nocturnal, being active at night. Many of them, and butterflies too, are equipped with coiled mouth parts of great length—long enough to reach the nectar supply at the base of a long floral tube.

Flower beetles rummage around in the flower clusters of many species, but are especially visible in members of the cactus and sunflower families. Transfer of pollen from anther to stigma of the same flower results in self pollination, that from one flower to another in cross pollination.

ABOUT COMMON SENSE

Thousands of visitors travel to Zion National Park each year. Each can see only a part of the floral display, that portion present during the visit. If each of the visitors picked even a solitary flower, the display of blossoms would be reduced and finally obliterated. Insects and birds would be deprived of some of their food supply and the plant species could not produce as many seeds. It is common sense, *backed by public law*, that one should *not* take plants or portions of plants in National Parks or Monuments. We occasionally mention edibility and medicinal use of some of the examples pictured and discussed, but such discussion should not be taken as either endorsement or encouragement for visitors to eat the plants or to use them for medicinal purposes. Some plants are poisonous when eaten or touched, and some of the poisonous ones resemble others that are edible. It is suggested that the visitor not learn survival techniques by eating wild plants in National Parks and Monuments. Few of the plants are truly edible, and those that are edible often have bad flavor or poor texture.

Aboriginal peoples ate about everything that could be eaten and spent most of their lives in search of food. The average visitor cannot expect to become proficient in the use of native plants during their visit to Zion.

The edible fruit in Zion National Park is that borne by the old orchard trees in the campgrounds.

UTAH YUCCA
YUCCA UTAHENSIS MCKELVEY
AGAVE FAMILY

Utah yucca is easily identified by its narrow, yellow green leaves and branching flower stalk. The leaves are often borne on a stem to as much as two feet long or more. The flowers are creamy white in color and are about two inches long. The plants grow well in sandy sites from lowest elevations in the Park to the summits of the highest plateaus. Seed pods dry at maturity and split open along lines of weakness, freeing hundreds of black wafer-like seeds. Flowering occurs from April at the lowermost elevations to June on the mesa tops.

DATIL YUCCA
YUCCA BACCATA TORR. IN EMORY
AGAVE FAMILY

This was the single most important wild plant
to prehistoric Indians of the Southwest. The long,
strong leaf fibers, obtained by soaking the leaves
in water and then pounding with a mallet, were
used for ropes, mats, sandals, baskets, cloth, and
thread. The flower stalk has been used as a fire
spindle to generate coals for starting fires. The
fruit of the datil yucca ripens as a fleshy sweet
berry, from which a sweet soup was made by
Indians. Produced in springtime, yucca flowers
are pollinated by small moths, who gather pollen
and pack it into crevices in the stigma. The moths
then lay eggs on the ovary. The eggs hatch into
larvae that burrow into the ovary where they
eat a portion of two of the six rows of seeds prior
to maturing as pupae. The pupae later develop
into adult moths.

ZION DAISY
ERIGERON SIONIS CRONQ.
ASTER FAMILY

Zion daisy is a plant of seeps, wet walls, and more commonly of hanging garden assemblages. The lower leaves are often lobed, and the plants spread by strawberry-like stolons, stems that grow from the plant base, touch the wet surface, and produce roots. When the stolon breaks, the newly rooted stem tip grows still other stems that spread. Overlapping stolons finally form a small mat on the wet stone. From this mat arises the flowering stems with their attractive white flowers. Zion daisy belongs to a category of plants called narrow endemics; that is, the plants are known only from a specific area. Zion daisy grows only in Zion Canyon and nearby vicinity. The scientific name was spelled "*sionis*" because there is no letter "z" in Latin. Main flowering time is springtime and early summer, but flowering continues into the autumn.

THOMPSON ERIOGONUM
ERIOGONUM THOMPSONAE WATS.
BUCKWHEAT FAMILY

This is a plant of fine textured soils such as occur on portions of the Chinle and Moenave formations in Zion Canyon proper. The plants are locally common on the Chinle in the Petrified Forest section of the Park. The flattopped flower clusters are produced in late summer, with the white, cream, or less commonly sulfur yellow flowers displayed in September and October. The plants vary in stem development, with some phases almost lacking an elongate leafy stem, but others have a long leafy stem. Plants of the genus *Eriogonum* tend to grow only on specific soil types. There are numerous species in Utah.

SPIDER MILKWEED
ASCLEPIAS ASPERULA (DECNE.) WOODSON
MILKWEED FAMILY

Greenish to cream flowers of this milkweed set it apart at once from other milkweed species. Borne in hemispheric clusters, the flowers produce nectar at the base of the corona (crown) of hornlike appendages that arise from the base of the petals. Insects in search of nectar for food trample the flower and by chance get their feet caught in the clip mechanism that holds the masses of pollen (pollinia) tightly in adjacent anther sacs. The pollinia are carried to the surface of the stigma of other flowers. There the large number of pollen grains germinate at once to fertilize the numerous ovules in the ovary. The familiar milkweed pod is the result. This plant is scattered in much of the Park. Flowering occurs in springtime.

EMORY SEEPWILLOW
BACCHARIS EMORYI GRAY IN TORR.
SUNFLOWER FAMILY

This is a common streamside plant in Zion Canyon, where it grows with Fremont cottonwood, boxelder, and velvet ash. A second species, *Baccharis glutinosa* Pers. or sticky seepwillow, is also present in the canyon. It differs from Emory seepwillow in having less numerous flower clusters near the end portion of the stem. Both species have sexes on separate plants; that is, there are male plants and female plants. Only the female plants produce seed and only cross pollination is possible. Flowers are borne in spring, summer, and autumn. The longer silvery pappus of the female heads often constitutes the showy part of the plants.

This plant is a near relative of Eaton daisy, but differs in its conspicuous narrow leaves with a waxy covering giving a bluish appearance. Plants grow in crevices in sandstone, especially in the Navajo Formation, which is easily visited in the Clear Creek Canyon portion of the Park east of the tunnel. Flower color varies from white to pinkish or lavender. Daisies generally bloom in the spring, which helps in distinguishing them from the usually fall flowering asters. They tend also to have many more ray flowers than the asters.

TUFTED EVENING-PRIMROSE OR MORNING-LILY
OENOTHERA CAESPITOSA NUTT.
EVENING-PRIMROSE FAMILY

This beautiful large flowered perennial herb has all of its leaves at the base of the plant. The stem between the leaves does not elongate, and both flowers and leaves form a compact tuft, hence the common name. Flowers open in the evening, remain open through the night and close by midmorning. Often the flowers open for a second night, but typically they have taken on a pinkish hue, and when finally closed, the drying flowers are a rich rose. The blossoms are readily seen in early morning, hence the name morning-lily for the large lily-like flowers. The plants are likely to occur on gravelly slopes and benchlands, but also grow on fine textured formations such as the Chinle and Moenkopi. Springtime and early summer are main times of flowering.

PALE EVENING-PRIMROSE
OENOTHERA PALLIDA LINDL.
EVENING-PRIMROSE FAMILY

Flowers of evening-primrose species have the appearance of dainty handkerchiefs. The petals are plaited, indicating where they were folded when contained within the bud. Fragrance and the white flowers make the plants readily apparent at night when they are visited by hawkmoths and other night flying insects. The pale evening-primrose has stems elongated between the leaves, and the flowers are displayed near the stem apex, some distance above the ground. Pollen grains cling together like strings of beads, which adorn the heads of the moth visitors. Mainly, this plant grows in sandy soil, which is abundant in this land of sandstone. Flowering is mainly in springtime and early summer, but some flowers are displayed throughout the growing season.

BLUE ELDERBERRY
SAMBUCUS CAERULEA RAF.
HONEYSUCKLE FAMILY

This plant is known for its showy flattopped flower clusters, compound leaves, and weak stems with a thick spongy pith. The dark blue-black fruits often appear bluish due to a covering of wax. The ripe fruits are edible, but tart, and are much prized for making jelly, pie, syrup, or even wine. The species occurs sporadically through much of middle and higher elevation portions of the Park. The stems tend to grow in rounded clumps mainly six to ten feet in height. Flowers are produced primarily during the summer season. In autumn the heavy fruiting clusters tend to bend downward. They are most tasty following an autumn frost.

Edible bulbs of the sego lily, which taste not unlike a small potato, were eaten by pioneers and by Indians. Harvesting of bulbs is difficult. The species is widespread but nowhere abundant in the Park. A second species, *Calochortus flexuosus* Wats., grows in lower elevation portions of Zion National Park. It has zigzag stems that sometimes trail along the ground and lavender flowers. Sego lily is the state flower of Utah, a tribute to its use by pioneers of the state. Persons untrained in the difference between sego lily and death camas have been known to mistake the two. Sego lily produces only one or two leaves per plant, and these trail ribbon-like over the ground. Death camas has a cluster of v-shaped leaves that stand erect or ascending from the bulb. The flowers of the two are remarkably different. Both are displayed in springtime.

FALSE SOLOMON-SEAL
SMILACINA STELLATA (L.) DESF.
LILY FAMILY

There are two species of *Smilacina* in Zion National Park. The one named above is the more common of the two. It has a simple flower cluster, a raceme, with several white starlike flowers. The second species, *Smilacina racemosa* (L.) Desf., has a branched flower cluster, a panicle, with numerous tiny cream flowers. Both species grow best in shady moist sites. The plants are mainly from one to two feet in height. Hanging gardens often have clusters of at least one of the species growing at their bases. The plants flower in April and May.

Members of the mustard family are among the most easily recognized of any of the plant families. The flowers have four sepals, four petals, four long and two short stamens, and a fruit that opens at maturity with a central membranous partition persisting where the seeds were attached. Many members of the family have yellow flowers, but wedgeleaf is an exception (among many). This is a small annual that occurs on sandy or gravelly soils at all elevations in the Park. Flowers open in early springtime.

WATERCRESS
NASTURTIUM OFFICINALE R. BR. IN AIT.
MUSTARD FAMILY

This plant grows in water, usually in slow moving streams or in springs. An excellent salad plant with a peppery taste, it is also a good potherb and is sometimes used for flavoring soups and meats. Plants gathered in the wild pose potential health hazards due to possible contamination of the water by infectious organisms. Flowers are produced in summer, following active growth after quiescence in the cold of winter. The plant is presumed to have been introduced from Europe by pioneer settlers. A good place to view this plant is in the swamp along the Gateway to the Narrows Trail.

FRAGRANT SAND-VERBENA
ABRONIA FRAGRANS NUTT. EX HOOK.
FOUR O'CLOCK FAMILY

This plant grows in sandy sites in Zion Canyon, where its flower clusters with rounded tops waft fragrance on the desert air. It is often unnecessary to stoop to detect the delightful odor of this plant. The family has received its name from the propensity of many members to open in the late afternoon or early evening. The flowers remain open through the night, and both color and odor serve to attract hawkmoths, which have a long tubular mouth part for extracting nectar from the long flowers, and, coincidentally, pollinating them. Glands on the plant parts secrete sticky substances and sand grains adhere to the surfaces. When rain falls the flower clusters nod, protecting their open faces by being sheltered by broad bracts at the cluster base. The plants flower from early springtime to autumn.

ANGELS-TRUMPET

DATURA WRIGHTII REGEL
POTATO FAMILY

This species has the largest flowers of any plant
in southern Utah and vicinity. The flowers are
commonly five to seven inches long and as broad
or broader. White is the typical color, but shades
of lavender and blue are sometimes present at
the lobe tips. The flowers are sweetly scented,
in contrast to the odor of the leaves, which smell
like a wet dog. The plants contain a number of
complex chemical compounds called alkaloids,
which are poisonous singly or in combination.
Some of the alkaloids are used as drugs to treat
various ailments—headaches, for example. The
plant is to be viewed for its imposing beauty,
but avoided because of its toxicity. The species
is also known as sacred datura, moonlily, and
Jimson weed (a contraction of Jamestown weed).
Plants occur mainly at low elevations in the Park
and flower from late spring through autumn.

STINKING MILKVETCH OR RATTLEWEED
ASTRAGALUS PRAELONGUS SHELDON
LEGUME FAMILY

This large milkvetch is easy to detect and identify, even from some distance, due to its rank, disagreeable odor. The odor is derived from the element selenium, which the plant obtains from the selenium bearing soils in which it grows. The element is used in certain chemical processes within the plant, where it is substituted for its sister element sulfur. Selenium in the plant imparts a poisonous quality, and when the plant is consumed by grazing animals, they are poisoned. Death of livestock can ensue within a few hours following eating of the plant, or the animal might suffer for weeks or months prior to dying. The species is common on fine textured, typically varicolored outcrops of the Chinle and Moenkopi formations. Flowering is in springtime. Plants can be seen along the Watchman Trail.

NUTTALL GILIA
LINANTHASTRUM NUTTALLII (GRAY) EWAN
PHLOX FAMILY

Nuttall gilia is a plant of crevices in Navajo
Sandstone and other formations, but occurs less
commonly in other sites also. The rounded
clumps, to about a foot in height, and white to
creamy 5-lobed flowers resemble phlox. The
yellow anthers in the flower's center, appearing
like a yellow eye, make the distinction from phlox
easy. When in full bloom the plants are especially
showy, the beauty added to by the setting on
buff sandstone. Flowering is in springtime. The
plants are common on sandstone in much of the
Park.

PRICKLY POPPY
ARGEMONE MUNITA DUR. & HILG.
POPPY FAMILY

The showy large flowers of this prickly plant resemble fried eggs, sunny side up, the yolk being a large cluster of yellow anthered stamens and the white the spreading petals. The sap of the plant is milky, often white or yellow, and when the plant is injured the milky sap exudes from the wound. The sap becomes black upon drying, giving the plant a rather beaten appearance in age. The plant parts and sap contain alkaloids, which have been investigated by drug companies. Prickly poppy grows in sandy soil, often along roadsides, at lower elevations mainly. Watch for it along the Kolob Terrace Road, where it flowers from early summer to early autumn.

UTAH SERVICEBERRY
AMELANCHIER UTAHENSIS KOEHNE
ROSE FAMILY

This intricately branched rounded shrub is common to abundant in many sections of the Park. It grows intermixed in the pinyon-juniper woodland and in the ponderosa pine community. The leaves are oval, with a few small teeth at the apex. The flowers are borne in springtime as the leaves expand, with the small apple-like fruits (pomes) developing later. The fruit is consumed by birds and other animals, but is too dry, bland, and seedy for more than passing human consumption. The larger fruited, *Amelanchier alnifolia* (Nutt.) Nutt. (shadbush or Saskatoon), is also present in the Park. Its fruit is much more juicy and is more palatable to people. Serviceberry wood is very tough and hard when dried. Indians used it for digging sticks, and made use of thin long straight stems for arrow shafts.

POISON IVY
TOXICODENDRON RYDBERGII (SMALL) GREENE
CASHEW FAMILY

Poison ivy in the west is a shrub; it does not become a climbing vine as in the east. The combination of alternate leaves, each with three coarsely toothed leaflets, and white to creamy berries provide identifying characters. The plant contains the substance urushiol, which causes severe dermatitis in sensitive people. *Do not consider yourself to be insensitive to this poisonous substance*! Sensitivity varies from person to person and with conditions of health and age of each individual. Don't touch the plant to see if you are sensitive. Minor contact yields coarse lesions, which form scabs after a few days. The scabs often crack and bleed and serve as a points of entry for secondary infections. The plants grow in moist areas through much of the lower elevation portions of the Park. Be observant when walking in such areas.

THOMPSON PETERIA
PETERIA THOMPSONAE WATS.
LEGUME FAMILY

The Thompson peteria was named in honor of
Ellen Powell Thompson, sister of John Wesley
Powell, who first collected the plant near Kanab,
Utah in 1872. The species, with its creamy flowers
in long racemes, resembles some species of
Astragalus. However, the sharply spiny paired
stipules (leaflike appendages) at the base of each
leaf mark it at once as different from all *Astragalus*
species in Utah. *Peteria* is widely distributed in
southern Utah and Nevada. In the Park, it is
common along the Watchman Trail where it
grows in small to large clumps and blooms in
May and June.

Inflated stems of this curious plant mark it for easy identification. The plants grow quickly in springtime and the fresh green stems soon expand along the internodes below the main branches. Often the secondary branches are inflated also. When young and tender the swollen portions of the stem can be eaten. The flavor is not unlike rhubarb, another plant in the buckwheat family. The tartness is due to the presence of oxalic acid in the plant sap. Tiny cream to yellowish flowers are borne in open clusters at the summit of the branches in spring, summer, and early autumn. Stems persist throughout the winter. Watch for this plant on low elevation portions of the Park.

This tall thistle, with its candelabra arrangement of heads and white to cream flower heads, is a biennial. The stalks grow quickly in the spring of the second year of their existence elevating the flower heads to 3 feet or more above the ground. When flowering is completed and seed has drifted away the plant dies, but it stands wand-like for a time, marking the place where it grew and displayed its beauty. The rosette of leaves from which next year's flowering stem will develop appears gray green, tightly hugging the dry ground. These plants are most readily seen in lower elevation portions of the Park blooming in springtime. Other thistles are present also, but none will exactly match this species.

OLD MAN OR SAND SAGEBRUSH
ARTEMISIA FILIFOLIA TORR.
Sunflower Family

The filiform (threadlike) divisions of the leaves make this plant easy to identify. It is a large grayish or silvery sagebrush of sandy low elevation sites in Zion. The foliage has the odor of sagebrush. Flower clusters are branched, and the tiny cream flowers are borne in late summer or autumn. Distinctive confluent (blended into one) yellow anthers protrude from the flowers giving them a yellowish appearance. Two herbaceous species of *Artemisia*, known as terragon (*Artemisia dracunculus* L.) and Louisiana wormwood (*Artemisia ludoviciana* Nutt.), grow in Zion National Park. They occupy sandy sites along the Virgin River flood plain and on canyon slopes and uplands. The common name sagebrush is usually confined to the shrubby members. Flowering of this species is in late summer and autumn.

BIG OR COMMON SAGEBRUSH
ARTEMISIA TRIDENTATA NUTT.
SUNFLOWER FAMILY

The scientific name of big sagebrush is derived from the three-toothed leaves. This is a very common shrub in much of the west where it occupies thousands of square miles. Lands dominated by this plant and by various bunch-grasses were cleared for farmland in Utah and elsewhere. Although the flavor is poor, and the plants are seldom preferred by cattle, sheep and wildlife, it is still a principal food plant for these animals during critical portions of each year. The plants recover well after fire and serve to hold the soil from excessive erosion. Some of the plants in deep alluvial soils, as along Coalpits Wash, reach a height of 8 feet or more. Dried wood burns with a hot fragrant fire. The species was used as a principal source of medicine by Indians, who used it to treat almost all of their ailments, physical and spiritual. It flowers in autumn.

Dwarf mountain mahogany, *Cercocarpus intricatus*, is only one of three species of mountain mahogany known from Zion. It is a crevice plant in Navajo Sandstone and is readily seen along the road east of the tunnel in Clear Creek Canyon. The leaves of *Cercocarpus intricatus* and *C. ledifolius* Nutt., the curlleaf mountain mahogany, are both ever-green, but those of *C. ledifolius* are much the larger (mainly 1/2 to 1 1/2 inches long). Those of *C. intricatus* are often less than half an inch long. Alder-leaf mountain mahogany, *C. montanus* Raf., has deciduous leaves. Flowers of all species are small and lack petals. The fruit consists of long tailed hairy achenes, which are conspicuous, especially when back lighted, in autumn. Wood of all species is very hard and very heavy. It was used by Indians for digging sticks. The plants flower in springtime.

ROCK SPIRAEA
PETROPHYTUM CAESPITOSUM (NUTT.) RYDB.
ROSE FAMILY

Also known as rockplant or rockmat, this plant is adequately named both scientifically and commonly; it clings mat-like to rock surfaces or sometimes hangs free from overhanging cliffs or in hanging gardens. It is a shrub despite its low growth, and is related to the spiraeas grown in home flower gardens. The numerous blossoms crowd each other along the erect flowering stem in autumn. Stems of previous years ornament the mat of glossy silvery green leaves. Watch for this plant on rock surfaces throughout the Park.

BLUE FLAX
LINUM PERENNE L.
FLAX FAMILY

The native blue flax is considered by some botanists as ssp. *lewisii* (Pursh) Hulten, or Lewis flax; it is named in honor of Lewis of the Lewis and Clark expedition. Bright blue petals displayed in morning during summer on wand-like stems are the trademark of this flax. However, the phase of the species in lower elevation portions of Zion has pure white petals, so the usual common name is a misnomer. The petals hardly persist for a day; even gentle breezes cause them to fall, and the ground is often strewn with them by midmorning. Some Indians cooked the oily flax seeds, which might also contain a substance that yields cyanide upon digestion. Beware of using the seeds for food, unless cooked thoroughly. Fibers from flax stems are the source of linen and were used for cordage.

Appearing like tiny eyes, the flower clusters of
rattlesnake weed seem to peer from the prostrate
mats. Blue green foliage and the startling white-
bracted cyathia, which resemble flowers, make
a strong contrast in an arid setting. The petal-
like bracts and cup-like cyathia bear male and
female flowers, each stalked. The female flower
is reduced to a three-lobed ovary, the male flower
to a solitary stamen. Both arise from the base
of the cyathium and the ovary commonly bends
over the margin of the cyathium. A nectar gland
is borne on the margin of the cyathium also. This
together with the flowers, cyathium, and white
bracts form a structure that functions like a
flower. Watch for this plant in lower elevation
dry regions of the Park. It flowers in springtime.

CREEPING MAHONIA OR OREGON GRAPE
MAHONIA REPENS (LINDL.) G. DON
BARBERRY FAMILY

Creeping mahonia grows as an understory plant in most plant communities in Zion. The compound leaves with thick leathery, spine-margined leaflets are features that make identification easy. Attractive spring borne bright yellow flowers based on the number three (i.e. 3 or 6 sepals, and 6 petals) are also distinctive. The fruit consists of blue black berries with not very pleasant flavor eaten fresh. However, the berries have been used to make wine, and jams and jellies especially when mixed with other fruits.

FREMONT MAHONIA
MAHONIA FREMONTII (TORR.) FEDDE
BARBERRY FAMILY

This plant has bluish to purplish green leaves due to a waxy covering on the epidermis. The wax acts to protect the plant from excessive water loss, a requirement made necessary by the dry habitats in which the plant grows. Individual plants tend to have a single main trunk, which develops branches low down and forms a rounded crown, like a miniature tree. The numerous flower clusters stain the plant bright yellow in springtime. Fruit is about half an inch in length, thin walled, hollow, and often open at the terminal end prior to maturity. When ripe the red to purple fruit is tart and of pleasant flavor. Fruits are eaten by coyotes and fox, who serve to distribute the seeds over wide areas. This plant can be seen in the Petrified Forest sector.

Three species of *Lithospermum* grow in Zion: a
low growing large flowered species, showy
stoneseed; a taller species with rather inconspicuous pale greenish yellow flowers, *L. ruderale*
Dougl. ex Lehm. or contra stoneseed; and *L.
multiflorum* Torr., or pretty stoneseed, with its
conspicuous yellow to yellow orange flowers. The
name stoneseed comes from the appearance of
the four stone-like nutlets that comprise the fruit
of each flower. The contra stoneseed derives its
common name from the use by Indians in Nevada
of this plant as a contraceptive. From observa-
tions of such use, drug companies made inves-
tigations and developed modern birth control
pills. Watch for this plant in the ponderosa pine
zone especially. It flowers from early springtime
to past midsummer.

This beautiful plant of hanging gardens and stream and seep margins is the larger of the Zion columbines. The spurs of the flowers, from which the name *Aquilegia* (from the similarity of the spur talons of the eagle, *Aquila)* is derived, are sufficiently long that only the very long mouth parts of hawkmoths and butterflies can reach the nectar supplies at the base inside. Pollinators of columbine flowers are not especially selective on a species by species basis, often visiting the flowers of one species and then another, especially when the species grow nearby or intermixed. Cross pollination between the species results in seeds that grow into hybrid plants. Such hybrids are formed between the two species in Zion and many intermediate specimens are present. Watch for them in the wet areas of the Park's low elevations in early summer.

WESTERN COLUMBINE
AQUILEGIA FORMOSA FISCH. IN DC.
BUTTERCUP FAMILY

The flowers of western columbine are red and yellow; spurs and sepals are red and the petal blades are yellow. The powderpuff cluster of yellow stamens protruding from the front of the flower and the graceful backward protruding spurs give the flower the appearance of flight. In a fanciful way, they appear like small colorful birds. Hummingbirds are known to visit the flowers of this plant, and less commonly also those of the golden columbine. The Foster phase (*Aquilegia formosa* var *fosteri* Welsh) of the western columbine is known only from Zion. It is distinguished by having more finely divided leaves and by having sticky glands overall, and usually grows as a crevice plant at moderate elevations in the Park. Both phases flower in early summer.

BERRY PRICKLYPEAR
OPUNTIA PHAEACANTHA ENGELM
Cactus Family

This is the most conspicuous of Zion's several pricklypears. Its flowers are yellow to apricot, often streaked with red or orange. The stem joints can be huge, to a foot or more long and about as broad. The fruit ripens to a reddish or purplish berry (tuna), which is edible when ripe and can be made into excellent jelly and pancake syrup. The fruits were a seasonal staple in the diets of all Indians who lived where they grow. Zion's other pricklypear species have flowers that vary from yellow to orange, pink, or magenta. Flowering occurs in May and June. See the plains pricklypear for discussion of hybrids.

WHIPPLE CHOLLA
OPUNTIA WHIPPLEI ENGELM. & BIGEL.
CACTUS FAMILY

The stems of cholla cactus species serve the plants in many ways, in preservation and storage of water, in support, and in food manufacture. The stems provide less surface area than do ordinary leaves, thus reducing water loss. A thick waxy covering on the stems likewise reduces loss of water. Cells within the stem hold water tightly bound to thin strands of protein; the water is not available for drinking by humans. The stored water and food is protected from grazing animals by strong sharp spines, which are additional modified leaves. Fruit is fleshy, and has been eaten by Indians boiled, with squash. These plants can be seen near the visitor center (where planted), on the trail to the Petrified Forest, and along the road to the Kolob Terrace. Flowers are borne in early summer.

ARROWLEAF BALSAMROOT
BALSAMORHIZA SAGITTATA (PURSH) NUTT.
SUNFLOWER FAMILY

This plant is easily recognized by its grayish hairy leaves with arrow shaped blades to several inches in length and flower heads not unlike sunflowers. The species grows widely over the western part of the United States, but in Zion National Park it is present mostly on the plateau summits, mainly in meadows. The flowers and other plant parts have the odor of balsam, and the roots exude a yellowish resin. Indians used the plant medicinally for various ailments and ground the roots for food. The bright yellow heads are borne in springtime.

DESERT MARIGOLD
BAILEYA MULTIRADIATA HARV. & GRAY
SUNFLOWER FAMILY

The white to silvery stems and leaves and bright yellow many rayed heads of flowers atop almost naked stems to more than a foot tall are characteristic for this *Baileya* alone among the numerous sunflower genera native to Zion. A second species, *Baileya pleniradiata* Harv & Gray, is known from Zion also. Its ray flowers are less then half an inch in length while those of *multiradiata* are more than half an inch. The leafless portion of the stem, which supports the flower head, is less than three inches long in *pleniradiata* and more than that length in *multiradiata*. The plants grow best in gravelly sites, and flower profusely in springtime but in some years produce their bright flowers year round. The Zion vicinity is the northernmost locality for these southern species in Utah.

RUBBER RABBITBRUSH
CHRYSOTHAMNUS NAUSEOSUS (PALLUS) BRITT.
SUNFLOWER FAMILY

The clusters of bright yellow flowers atop numerous stems of grayish leaved shrubs to 3 feet tall or more mark the autumn scene along roadsides and other naturally or man made disturbed areas over much of the west. Zion is no exception, and autumn scenes in the park are made more vivid by this beautiful shrub. However, the foliage is aromatic, the aroma not altogether pleasing to the human nose, hence the scientific name — derived from the same source word as nauseous. The plants produce a rubbery latex, from which rubber can be made. It was investigated as a source of this substance during World War II, when the supply of natural rubber fell into Japanese control.

BUSH ENCELIA
ENCELIA FRUTESCENS (GRAY) GRAY
SUNFLOWER FAMILY

White stems, rounded rough leaves to about an inch long, and bright orange-yellow rays serve to identify this rounded shrub. This species is rather widely distributed in southern Utah. It is also known from southern Nevada, Arizona, and California. The plants grow scattered in the desert shrubland of lower elevation portions of the Park. Watch for it along the Watchman Trail, where it flowers during late and early summer.

BROOM SNAKEWEED
GUTIERREZIA SAROTHRAE BRITT. & RUSBY
SUNFLOWER FAMILY

The genus *Gutierrezia* has several other common names, including matchweed, matchbrush, and broomweed. Two species grow in Zion. *Gutierrezia microcephala* (DC.) Gray or thread snakeweed is typically a taller plant with very narrow few-flowered heads. It grows best on volcanic materials in the Coalpits wash vicinity. Broom snakeweed is almost universal in low and middle elevation portions in many plant communities. The many fine dead twigs mingled with the live ones are an identifying mark. The plants are not eaten, even by rats and mice. When several mice were put into a cage and fed only snakeweed they turned to cannibalism and finally starvation without eating this plant. Both species flower in autumn.

BROOM GROUNDSEL
SENECIO SPARTIOIDES T. & G.
SUNFLOWER FAMILY

In late summer and autumn, broom groundsel flowers in sandy sites with goldenaster and rabbitbrush. Together, they stain the landscape yellow, except for the purples of hoary aster with which they grow. Broom groundsel is either single stemmed or more commonly clump-forming. The flower heads are elevated to form a flattopped cluster. Coincidence of flowering results in a yellow mass that lasts for a few days to a few weeks. *Senecio* is derived from the same word as senile, indicating age, from the gray hairy or hoary stems of some species. Although seldom eaten even when present in great abundance, animals are poisoned when they eat this plant. The species is especially abundant in Cave Valley.

GOLDENASTER
HETEROTHECA VILLOSA (PURSH) SHINN.
SUNFLOWER FAMILY

Goldenaster is almost a trademark of Zion, since the species have an affinity for sandy soils. There are at least three different phases of goldenaster in Zion, the common hoary goldenaster (named above) that grows on sandy soils in much of the Park, Zion goldenaster (*Heterotheca zionensis* Semple), a plant of deep sands in Cave Valley on the Park's west side, and a third sprawling slickrock kind especially from sandstone on the west side of the Park. The plants begin to bloom in springtime, and some of them continue flowering until late autumn, or even into the winter.

GOATSBEARD
TRAGOPOGON DUBIUS SCOP.
SUNFLOWER FAMILY

Goatsbeard is a literal translation of the Greek words for goat and beard. Tragedy has a similar derivation, except the second word in Greek is odos, a song. Goat song was the name applied to sad Greek plays during antiquity, hence tragedy. The beard of this attractive plant with dandelion-like flower heads atop a stem with narrow leaves derives from the expanded pappus (a highly modified calyx) atop the achenes (fruit) in the maturing head. The rays fall away and the apex of the fruit elongates, elevating the greatly enlarged pappus upward. The rays of the pappus spread, forming a parasol that supports the achene on rising air. If a weed is to gain a place, let it have beauty; certainly this plant is twice beautiful — once in flower and again in fruit. Flowering is mainly in summer.

YELLOW CAMISSONIA
CAMISSONIA MULTIJUGA (WATS.) RAVEN
EVENING-PRIMROSE FAMILY

This evening-primrose blooms during the day, mainly in springtime but sometimes also again in the autumn. The flowers are open sufficiently early and late that they are still visited by hawkmoths and other night flying insects, but they are also pollinated by bees and other insects during daytime, a kind of insurance policy. Larvae of hawkmoths, the familiar green hornworms that eat our tomato and potato plants, feed on this day bloomer as well as on the night blooming members of the family. Yellow camissonia is most commonly seen in Zion along the lower slopes of the Watchman Trail, and is easily identified by its distinctive deeply and irregularly cleft grayish leaves. The 4 sepals, 4 petals, and 8 stamens are distinctive for the family.

BLACKBRUSH
COLEOGYNE RAMOSISSIMA TORR.
ROSE FAMILY

Low elevation portions of the Park are clothed
by low rounded shrubs of blackbrush, a name
well applied to this shrub. Leaves are opposite
and the flowers seldom have petals. The four
yellow sepals serve in place of showy petals to
attract pollinators. Despite the opposite leaves
and four petals, the plants belong to the rose
family, which traditionally has the flowers based
on the number five and leaves that are alternate.
Deer are known to eat this plant in winter. Watch
for this plant in the Petrified Forest sector of the
Park, where it flowers in springtime.

FOURWING SALTBUSH
ATRIPLEX CANESCENS PURSH
GOOSEFOOT FAMILY

This is the least salt tolerant of the saltbush species in Utah. It receives its common name from the wing-like outgrowths of the paired bracts that enclose the fruit. Plants tend to be either exclusively male or exclusively female. However, there are some flowers of the other sex on plants that are mostly male or female, and there is a tendency for more male or female flowers to be produced in dry than in wet years. This plant grows well on sandy soils throughout the West. The leaves and stems are eaten by cattle, sheep, and wildlife. The fourwinged bracts are formed in the autumn, but persist on the plant for some months or even years. The inconspicuous flowers are produced in springtime. This shrub can be seen on the terraces near the visitor center.

MADDER
RUBIA TINCTORIA L.
MADDER FAMILY

Madder has been used to make a red dye, both in this country and in Europe. The plant is naturalized as an escape from cultivation, and it grows in the lower elevation portions of Zion Canyon. The fruit is fleshy and turns black at maturity. The leaves are armed with coarse recurved hairs that catch on clothes or animals. Bedstraw or *Galium* is another genus of this family that is native to Zion Canyon. There are at least seven species of *Galium* growing naturally in the Park. Some of these were used by pioneer families to stuff pillows and mattresses because of their softness and fragrance. Watch for herbs with whorled (several leaves per stem node) leaves throughout the park; they are the *Galium* species. The small greenish or yellowish flowers of madder are produced in early summer and beyond.

GLOBEMALLOW
SPHAERALCEA GROSSULARIIFOLIA (H. & A.) RYDB.
MALLOW FAMILY

Species of globemallow are easily identified by their orange (grenadine) petals and numerous stamens joined by their filaments around the styles, resembling tiny hollyhock flowers. No other genus of plants has this combination of features. The leaves and stems are covered by architecturally beautiful branched hairs, which give the plant a rough feeling. The fruit breaks apart at maturity, resulting in wedge shaped segments, each with a single seed. The sides of each segment have small windows of translucent material. The shape and number of windows are different for each species. There are at least three species of *Sphaeralcea* in the Park. All flower abundantly in springtime, and some of them blossom again in autumn. They can be seen throughout the Park, especially at lower elevations.

ZION DRABA
DRABA ASPRELLA GREENE
Mustard Family

This is a very attractive annual or short lived perennial plant of sandy sites, especially east of the tunnel in Clear Creek Canyon, but also along the West Rim Trail. The phase restricted to the Park belongs to var. *zionensis* (C.L. Hitchc.) Welsh & Reveal. The flowers are produced in springtime, and where abundant they stain the scene with their bright yellow. One of the family names, *Cruciferae*, is derived from the Latin name for cross, in reference to the four petals arranged in cross-like fashion in the flowers of its members. Flowers are produced in early springtime.

WESTERN WALLFLOWER
ERYSIMUM ASPERUM (NUTT.) DC.
MUSTARD FAMILY

Sulfur yellow large flowers made more showy by being bunched together in a cluster of expanding buds is the hallmark of this wallflower species. The beauty of these plants is made the more striking by the backgound of buff sand or stone or of vegetation that lacks this startling hue. Some detect a lilac scent to the flowers. The plants grow from low to high elevations in the Park, and can be seen elsewhere in much of the West. Springtime is the season of flowering.

ROUNDLEAF BUFFALOBERRY
SHEPHERDIA ROTUNDIFOLIA PARRY
OLEASTER FAMILY

The berries of this buffaloberry are not edible to man, either raw or cooked. The berries, leaves, and young stems are all silvery due to a covering of curiously beautiful stalked hairs, each with an umbrella-like top of radiating branches. They are architecturally among the most beautiful of hairs in the plant kingdom. The berries of roundleaf buffaloberry are similar in structure, color, and texture to those of the related Russian olive, *Elaeagnus angustifolia* L., an introduced Old World tree that is established along watercourses in some parts of the Park, but is especially abundant along reaches of the Virgin River below the Park boundaries. Flowers open in February or March in most years and are seldom seen by visitors. This buffaloberry is a Colorado Plateau endemic; it grows best intermixed with pinyon and juniper and in mountain brush communities.

PRINCE'S PLUME
STANLEYA PINNATA (PURSH) BRITT.
MUSTARD FAMILY

This plant grows to 3 feet tall or more, with its yellow plume-like racemes of bright flowers forming a dazzling display on hillsides in springtime. It grows where selenium is present in the soil and uses the selenium in place of sulfur, as do other selenium requiring plants. Often the soils occupied are fine textured — clays or silts, but it also grows on sand where selenium occurs. Because of the selenium content, the plants are poisonous to livestock and humans. However, Indians reputedly ate the plant as a potherb, after boiling the plant and pouring off the water several times.

TREFOIL OR DEERCLOVER
LOTUS PLEBEIUS (BRANDEGEE) BARNEBY
LEGUME FAMILY

There are several species of the genus *Lotus* in the Park. All have yellow flowers with a reddish tinge on one side of the petals, and all turn reddish in age. Long-bracted trefoil, named above, has 3 or 4 leaflets borne on a short stalk (petiole), and has stems that tend to sprawl on sandy ground or on sandstone, where the plants grow in crevices. Utah trefoil, *Lotus utahensis* Ottley, forms upright clumps and has the 3 to 5 leaflets borne stalkless at the stem nodes. Deer and other animals feed on these plants. Flowering takes place in springtime.

CLIFFROSE
PURSHIA MEXICANA (D. DON) WELSH
ROSE FAMILY

Cliffrose is an evergreen shrub to about 10 feet tall. Bark is shreddy like that of a juniper. Leaves typically are 5 or more lobed and have a white crusty margin. Flowers are creamy white to yellowish and resemble those of a small rose, hence the common name. The greenery of the plant is often obscured when plants are in full bloom. White sentinels on a varicolored landscape are an indication of this species in springtime. The bark was used by Indians for coarse cordage and insulation. Fruit is similar to that of the mountain mahogany, but several are produced by each cliffrose flower. The plants can be seen in the Petrified Forest vicinity. Cliffrose is closely related to bitterbrush (see following page).

BITTERBRUSH
PURSHIA TRIDENTATA (PURSH) DC.
ROSE FAMILY

Bitterbrush is distinguished from cliffrose by its usually more spreading growth form, mostly 3-toothed leaves, and tailless achenes borne one per flower. Despite its name, the plant is eaten readily by deer especially, but is consumed by all classes of wildlife and livestock. Animals eat the plants at all seasons of the year, but winter is the time when this plant is most important as food. Flowers of bitterbrush are smaller and less readily seen than are those of cliffrose, but they are beautiful in full flower in springtime. The species can be seen in the ponderosa pine forests at mid to upper elevations.

SKUNKBUSH
RHUS AROMATICA AIT.
CASHEW FAMILY

The plant, when crushed, gives off a disagreeable
odor, hence its common and scientific names. The
small yellow flowers appear in early springtime
before the leaves are formed. The fruit is fleshy
and covered with yellowish glands, which impart
a sour flavor. Because of the tartness, the fruit
has been used to make cooling drinks. The wood
is pliable and tough when wet and was used by
Indians for basketry and cordage. This plant is
a relative of poison ivy, within whose family it
is included, but it is not poisonous to the touch.
The plants grow in dry to moist sites, but seldom
occur where it is really wet.

BUTTERFLY WEED
ASCLEPIAS TUBEROSA L.
MILKWEED FAMILY

Also known as orange milkweed, this plant puts on a dazzling array of bright clusters of flowers in spring and early summer. Butterflies, bees, and beetles are all attracted. Pollination is not simple because the pollen is not transferred grain by grain. Instead, the pollen is massed into flattened plates (pollinia) each containing thousands of grains. Massed pollen from adjacent anthers are attached by a clip device, which must be pulled free from the anthers on the feet or mouth parts of insects. The insect must be sufficiently large to pull the pollen free or it will be trapped in the flower. Once on the foot of an insect the mass of pollen is placed by chance on the stigma where all of the grains germinate at once, ensuring fertilization of the hundreds of ovules in the ovary of the flower. Watch for this plant in sandy sites at lower and middle elevations.

UINTA GROUNDSEL
SENECIO MULTILOBATUS T. & G.
SUNFLOWER FAMILY

Uinta groundsel is a widespread species in Utah, which flowers in springtime. It grows in pinyon-juniper, mountain brush, and ponderosa pine communities. The bright yellow flower heads and many lobed leaves mark this species. It is one of more than twenty species of groundsel in the state. Members of the genus *Senecio* are distinguished by the bracts around the heads being disposed mainly in one row. A short second row is apparent in some of the species. The species was first collected in Utah by John Charles Fremont in the Uinta Basin on the return portion of his second expedition in 1844. It can poison livestock.

GOLDEN PEA
THERMOPSIS MONTANA NUTT.
LEGUME FAMILY

Bright yellow large pea-like flowers are characteristic of this species. The flower clusters are borne on plants mainly 1 to 2 feet in height. Leaflets are three in number. Pods are straight and flattened, each with several to many flattened seeds. Blossoms are produced mainly in May and June at moderate elevations in the Park. The species is widespread in the western United States. Plants grow in meadows and in openings in the ponderosa pine community. Flowering is in springtime and early summer.

GOLDEN CRYPTANTH
CRYPTANTHA CONFERTIFLORA (GREENE) PAYSON
BORAGE FAMILY

Cryptantha is a large genus in Utah, with more than 50 species. Only two of the species have truly yellow flowers. Golden cryptanth is mainly a species of the Great Basin and Virgin River drainages in Utah. The yellow cryptanth grows mainly in the drainages of the Colorado River in eastern Utah. Other species of cryptanth have white flowers, or white flowers with yellow centers. Golden cryptanth grows in low dry places where it flowers in springtime. Watch for it along the Watchman Trail.

CARDINAL-FLOWER OR SCARLET LOBELIA
LOBELIA CARDINALIS L.
BELLFLOWER FAMILY

The blue-gray anthers and lovely velvety petals of the cardinal flower are borne in summer and on into autumn. The blossoms simulate those of the hummingbird flower (see page 77) in color and in pollinators. Habitat for this plant is in hanging gardens and in seeps, but occasionally it takes advantage of moisture in crevices in rocks. The roots and other plant parts were used by some Indians to treat syphilis and intestinal worms. However, the plant should be regarded as poisonous to humans. Overdoses of extracts of plant parts, including leaves and fruits, produce vomiting, paralysis, rapid and feeble pulse, and death in humans. The plant should be viewed for its exquisite beauty but avoided because of its potential danger.

CANAIGRE OR WILD RHUBARB
RUMEX HYMENOSEPALUS TORR.
BUCKWHEAT FAMILY

Canaigre is the most readily seen of the four species of Rumex in Zion. The large leaves emerge from sandy soil in early springtime. Stems grow to a height of about 3 feet, and masses of tiny flowers are arranged in a branching cluster to a foot long or more. Flowers consist of usually 6 greenish sepals, the inner 3 of which enlarge as the fruit begins to mature. The enlarged sepals, called either valves or wings, are typically suffused with red or red purple. The brightly colored valves are a half inch long or more when fully expanded. This plant will be found blooming in the spring; April and May. Its roots are thickened storage organs. They are laden with tannin and have been used for tanning of leather. The plants grow best in sandy sites at low elevations in the Park.

PURPLE TORCH OR ENGELMANN HEDGEHOG-CACTUS
ECHINOCEREUS ENGELMANNII (PARRY) LEM.
CACTUS FAMILY

This is a plant of desert shrub communities at low elevations in Zion National Park. The stems are commonly clustered and are up to about a foot high. Spine color varies from white to yellowish or blackish from plant to plant, but sometimes all of those spine colors are present on a single stem. Flower buds are borne on stem sides beneath the surface during late springtime. They rupture the tissues of the plant and can be seen very early in the season among the spines. The fruit is fleshy when mature and reputedly has a strawberry flavor. The plants flower in April and May.

CLARETCUP
ECHINOCEREUS TRIGLOCHIDIATUS ENGELM.
CACTUS FAMILY

Claretcup grows not only in the desert shrub communities but also in the pinyon-juniper and oak-ponderosa pine woodlands. Stems are almost always clustered, and sometimes there are a hundred or more stems in a great hemispheric mound. The waxy scarlet petals enclose bright yellow stamens and the protruding green stigma. Flowers are produced in early springtime, first appearing as tiny red dots where the buds burst through the tissues of the stem. Claretcup is pollinated mainly by hummingbirds rather than by bees and beetles as is usual for cacti. However, both bees and beetles occasionally visit the flowers for pollen and nectar, and undoubtedly they are effective in pollination.

PLAINS PRICKLYPEAR
OPUNTIA MACRORHIZA ENGELM.
Cactus Family

This pricklypear, whose jointed stems creep along the ground and root, produces red fleshy edible fruit. The joints ordinarily lack long spines such as are common in most other pricklypears, but they are armed with tiny clustered spinules called glochids. The glochids, which are difficult to see individually, have downward pointing minute barbules that hold the glochid in the skin. Even a gentle touch is sufficient to imbed dozens or hundreds of glochids in the skin, where they produce a burning sensation. Often one must let them wear out as the skin is worn away. Flower color is frequently yellow in Zion, but many plants will have violet or even orange flowers. Watch for this plant to be blooming in May and June throughout Zion National Park. Plains pricklypear is known to form hybrids with the Engelmann pricklypear.

ARIZONA THISTLE
CIRSIUM ARIZONICUM (GRAY) PETRAK
SUNFLOWER FAMILY

The beautiful heads of thistle flowers betray a softness not apparent in the spiny aspect of the plant itself. Disk flowers alone constitute the flower type in the heads, which are borne mainly in springtime. Later, the expanding fluffy pappus demonstrates the beautiful architecture associated with the umbrella device, the thistle down, that carries the seeds on air currents, often for great distances. Thistles of whatever color are pollinated by hummingbirds, but those with bright red or carmine flowers are most readily seen by the birds. Watch for this plant in dry areas throughout Zion. It is readily seen along the trail to the Zion Narrows.

HUMMINGBIRD FLOWER
ZAUSCHNERIA LATIFOLIA (HOOK.) GREENE
Evening-primrose Family

Hummingbird flower or trumpet is a very showy fall blooming cousin of the fuchsia. It makes bright splashes of orange-red along crevices in the slickrock portions of the Park, east and west. The roots are anchored in crevices where moisture collects during storms. Zion's is known as var. *garrettii* (A. Nels.) Hillend. It is the phase of this wide ranging species known from Utah and nearby areas.

COMMON PAINTBRUSH
CASTILLEJA CHROMOSA A. NELS.
FIGWORT FAMILY

Scarlet is the usual color for the flower cluster of this plant, but specimens with orange, yellow, or even violet are seen occasionally. Color of the clusters is not due to the corollas (united petals) as in other plants. It is due, instead, to the colorful bracts and sepals; the corolla is green or only inconspicuously suffused with red or other colors. Pollinators are easily guided to these showy plants, as are beginning students from universities, each of whom feels unjustifiably proud to take yet another specimen for a herbarium (place where dried plants are kept). The plants are scattered at lower elevation portions of the Park, where they flower in springtime.

EASTWOOD OR SLICKROCK PAINTBRUSH
CASTILLEJA SCABRIDA EASTW.
FIGWORT FAMILY

Some plants tend to be specifically adapted for growth in distinctive habitats. Eastwood paintbrush is such a plant. It grows almost exclusively in crevices, where water is concentrated during even moderate rainfall. This plant has been confused with the common paintbrush, but is easily distinguished by the long greenish corolla protruding beyond calyx and colorful bracts. Watch for it in the crevices of the switchback trail to Echo Canyon and east of the tunnel in Clear Creek. It blooms in springtime.

CARDINAL MONKEYFLOWER
MIMULUS CARDINALIS DOUGL. EX BENTH.
FIGWORT FAMILY

The corolla of the cardinal monkeyflower is more red orange than scarlet, but is easily seen and is visited by hummingbirds. The plants occur in hanging gardens and along streams below them. They produce blossoms in springtime, especially, but some flowering continues late into the summer. The plants are commonly 1 to 2 feet long and erect or curved at the base. The flowers are somewhat larger than those of the late summer and autumn blooming Eastwood monkeyflower, *Mimulus eastwoodiae* Rydb., that grows in the hanging gardens of eastern Utah. Viewed from the front, the flower bears a fancied resemblance to the face of a monkey.

EATON PENSTEMON
PENSTEMON EATONII GRAY
FIGWORT FAMILY

Also known as firecracker or scarlet-bugler, this penstemon grows widely over the southern portion of Utah and surrounding states. More than 60 species of *Penstemon* grow in Utah. Only four or five have scarlet flowers and only the Eaton penstemon among those has corolla tubes that do not flare at the mouth. It is among the most easily identified of the 15 species of *Penstemon* that grow in the Park. It is typical for species of the figwort or snapdragon family to have only 2 or 4 stamens in a flower, but those of *Penstemon* have 5 stamens (from the Greek penta and stemon), but the fifth stamen lacks an anther and is called a staminode. The staminode is often bearded and lies in the throat of the corolla opening. Flowering occurs in springtime.

JONES PENSTEMON
PENSTEMON X JONESII PENNELL
FIGWORT FAMILY

The Jones penstemon is a natural hybrid between smooth penstemon, *P. laevis* Pennell (see page 106) and *P. eatonii*. Flowers of smooth penstemon are lavender blue to blue and those of Eaton penstemon are scarlet. Those of Jones penstemon range in color from coral pink to ruby red and red violet or almost purple black. Presence of the hybrids indicate that hummingbirds must occasionally visit bee pollinated flowers, and bees visit those flowers ordinarily visited by birds, such as *P. eatonii*. Jones penstemon is found where the range of the two parental species overlap. Variation in flower color indicates not simply hybridization but continual back crossing of the hybrids to the parents. Watch for this beautiful plant on the east side of the Park, where it flowers in spring and early summer.

PALMER PENSTEMON
PENSTEMON PALMERI GRAY
FIGWORT FAMILY

One of the few penstemons with scented flowers, this one is worth stooping to smell. Color varies from almost white to deep pink, with darker guidelines on the lower lip. The corolla tube flares toward the throat and is sufficiently large to accommodate large bees who search for nectar and act as pollinators. The plants grow mainly in dry places, but often line dry wash bottoms where moisture from runoff of storms or snowmelt persists in the subsurface layers for much of the season. Leaves and stems are an ashy gray or whitish color due to a covering layer of wax that pervents water loss from these handsome plants. Flowers are borne in springtime and early summer.

UTAH PENSTEMON
PENSTEMON UTAHENSIS EASTW.
FIGWORT FAMILY

The earliest blooming of Zion's penstemons, the lovely ruby red flat-faced flowers are easily seen. The flat face of the flowers and the lower growth (usually less than 1.5 feet tall) easily distinguish this species from Eaton penstemon. Flowers of red penstemons have been used medicinally by some Indians, boiled and the solution used to wash burns. The wash is reputed to stop pain and promote healing. The plants can be seen in springtime along the Watchman Trail.

SCARLET GILIA
GILIA AGGREGATA (PURSH) SPRENGEL
PHLOX FAMILY

Also known as skyrocket, this is another of the small number of plants with scarlet flowers in Zion. The scarlet color, starlike flaring floral lobes, and odor of skunk distinguish this perennial herb at once. The flowers provide a rich source of nectar for hummingbirds who pollinate them. The floral tube is too narrow for most bees to penetrate to the nectar reward, so some of them have learned to cut a hole through the side near the tube base. The nectar is then stolen without any real benefit to the plant. Flowers of high elevation phases of scarlet gilia are often not scarlet at all. They can vary in color from pink to ruby red, orange, or white. Some of these have very long floral tubes and are pollinated primarily by night flying moths. Initial flush of flowering is in springtime, but some flowers are produced throughout the growing season.

LARGE FOUR O'CLOCK
MIRABILIS MULTIFLORA (TORR) GRAY IN TORR.
FOUR O'CLOCK FAMILY

A poet has said that "things are not what they seem." The poet could have had four o'clock in mind, because the colorful parts of the flower are probably sepals, not petals. One or the other of those floral parts is missing. The flowers are borne in dense heads within expanded sepal-like green bracts. Blossoms open in springtime and early summer one or a few at a time within each of numerous heads on the plant, sometimes obscuring the foliage with the numerous flowers. Opening of the flowers is stimulated by low light of late afternoon or during the day when clouds obscure the sun. Pollinators are aided in the search for the colorful flowers by a musky scent. The plants grow well from seeds, but do not transplant readily. Watch for them in the desert shrub and pinyon-juniper communities, where they flower from spring to autumn.

UTAH DAISY
ERIGERON UTAHENSIS GRAY
SUNFLOWER FAMILY

Utah daisy is a perennial herb with upright branches topped with blue, pink, or less commonly white rayed heads of flowers produced in springtime. The plant grows mainly in rock crevices, but often where there is some shade from an adjacent shrub or rock. It is one of a baker's dozen of species of the genus *Erigeron* to grow in the Park. Two of those species, the religious and Zion daisies, are restricted to the Park and nearby areas. The Zion daisy is discussed above. The religious daisy (*Erigeron religiosus* Cronq.) grows in sand throughout the Park, but is especially abundant along Clear Creek in the eastern portion of the region. It has white flowers and is a short lived perennial or biennial.

LEAN CLOVER
TRIFOLIUM MACILENTUM GREENE
LEGUME FAMILY

Lean clover grows mainly in the ponderosa pine community at middle to upper elevations in Zion. Watch for it in springtime among the oak thickets on the east side of the Park. The pale almost glassy pink petals are showy en masse. The plant occurs in places that have moisture in springtime, but which dry out as the heat of summer takes the water. The three leaflets are characteristic of many species of clover. Petals remain attached as they dry and enclose the developing fruit.

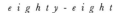

SEARLS PRAIRIE-CLOVER
DALEA SEARLSIAE (GRAY) BARNEBY
LEGUME FAMILY

Prairie clovers are distinguished by the dark glandular spots on the leaves and other plant parts, and by the spike-like racemes of small flowers, which are showy together when in full bloom. The plants are especially common along Watchman Trail and Petrified Forest sectors of the Park. Flowering is in May and June. The species is locally common in southwestern Utah and westward into Nevada.

FILAREE OR STORKSBILL
ERODIUM CICUTARIUM (L.) L'HER
GERANIUM FAMILY

This is one of the very early flowering plants in Zion. The bright 5-petaled flowers appear almost at ground level on plants grown from seeds that germinated following rains of the previous autumn. Soon the ovary elongates to form the familiar storksbill fruit, in reality a peculiar device consisting of 1-seeded structures that coil when dry and straighten when moist. The winding and unwinding action acts to bury the seed, guaranteeing germination when the soil is wet during the next autumn. The young plants have been eaten as a potherb and are reported to have been used medicinally.

MEXICAN MANZANITA
ARCTOSTAPHYLOS PUNGENS H.B.K.
HEATH FAMILY

This is the evergreen leathery leaved shrub of valley slopes with stems resembling the muscled torso of a professional athlete. Urn shaped whitish to bright pink flowers open in clusters near stem ends in early springtime. Shrubs vary in height from 3 to 9 feet (or rarely even more), intermixed with live oak, Gambel oak, and pinyon-juniper communities. A second species, greenleaf manzinita or *Arctostaphylos patula* Greene, grows in dense stands as understory in the ponderosa pine forest on the mesa tops. It blooms early also, and the typical visitor is unlikely to see it flowering during summer visits. Ordinarily it is a lower growing shrub, seldom over 5 feet tall.

MOUNTAIN SNOWBERRY
SYMPHORICARPOS OREOPHILUS GRAY
HONEYSUCKLE FAMILY

Two species of snowberry grow in Zion. The second species is the long-flower snowberry, *Symphoricarpos longiflorus* Gray. Short thick and long slender describe the flowers of the two species respectively. Neither is especially showy from a distance, but the structure of the individual flowers is added to by the pink to red purple coloration, producing subtle beauty in miniature. The plants are generally less than 3 feet tall and have opposite small leaves. Mountain snowberry is mainly a plant of higher elevations in the Park; long-flower snowberry is a shrub of hot dryish situations at lower elevations. Snowberry species flower in springtime and early summer.

COMMON ROCKCRESS
ARABIS PERENNANS WATS.
MUSTARD FAMILY

Rock cress species, four of them, are among the early flowering plants of Zion. Common rockcress often grows beneath shrubs and pokes its flower stalks up through the protective branches. When thus protected, the base of the plant is frequently woody. A rosette of leaves generally occupies a basal portion of the plant between branches of the flowering stem of the current year. The long slender fruit (silique) of this plant is either spreading or pendulous at maturity, giving a graceful structure to the plant in fruit. Other species of rockcress in the Park are *Arabis demissa* Greene (low rockcress), *A. holboellii* Hornem. (Holboell rockcress), and *A. pulchra* Jones (pretty rockcress). Watch for these species throughout the Park.

ZION MILKVETCH
ASTRAGALUS ZIONIS JONES
LEGUME FAMILY

This species was described and named by Marcus E. Jones almost a century ago from plants taken by him in Zion Canyon. Its sharply pointed leaflets, remnants of previous years' dead leaves, and brightly purple or red mottled curved pods are identifying features. The plant grows well in crevices but is also in the sandy canyon bottom soil in oakbrush and pinyon-juniper woods. Like other milkvetch species, this one produces blossoms in springtime. Watch for it along the trail to the Zion Narrows and in crevices in sandstone elsewhere.

ZION SWEETPEA
LATHYRUS BRACHYCALYX RYDB.
LEGUME FAMILY

The Zion phase of the species [var. *zionis* (C.L. Hitch.) Welsh] is a very common spring flowering plant in Zion Canyon. It grows as understory in oak and pinion-juniper communities. The large pink to lavender flowers are supported on weak stems that clamber over other vegetation or are supported by tendrils from the leaf tips. The tendrils clasp stems and leaves of other plants allowing the sweet pea to display its flowers above the vegetation. When the plants grow free from other species, as they often do, the tendrils of adjacent stems clasp others of the same or adjacent sweetpea plants adding strength to the common mass. The pale pinkish to whitish Lanszwert sweetpea (*Lathyrus lanszwertii* Kellogg) grows at high elevations in the Park, especially in aspen communities.

NEW MEXICO LOCUST
ROBINIA NEOMEXICANA GRAY
LEGUME FAMILY

Bright pink clusters of typical pea-like flowers on dwarf trees with spiny branches are the hallmark of New Mexico locust. The species in Utah is known only from Zion and from the western part of Washington County, which includes Zion National Park, where it flowers in late springtime. A tree sized specimen grows in back of the visitor center, and smaller ones by the parking lot at the Court of the Patriarchs. Watch for others along the road north of the Lodge. Plant parts are poisonous to livestock and to humans, although rarely fatal. Observe this beautiful plant but do not attempt to eat any part of it.

DESERT PHLOX
PHLOX AUSTROMONTANA COV.
PHLOX FAMILY

The flowers of desert phlox can be white, bluish, pink, or red violet, often all on the same plant simultaneously. The blooms of the Zion phase [var. *jonesii* (Wherry) Welsh] are mainly pink to almost red. The phlox forms cushiony mats, with numerous stems, that festoon ledges, cliffs, and slickrock. It grows on rocky slopes and ridges mostly in oakbrush and pinyon-juniper woods, but is sometimes found at higher elevations. Watch for this plant along the trails to Echo and Refrigerator Canyons, where it is showy in springtime.

ZION SHOOTING STAR
DODECATHEON PULCHELLUM (RAF.) MERR.
PRIMROSE FAMILY

This species occurs over much of western North America, but the Zion Canyon phase [var. *zionense* (Eastw.) Welsh] differs in its large thin leaves and large flowers from plants elsewhere in Utah and the West. The flowers nod and the petals are bent back giving the appearance of motion. The shooting-star similarity is further added to by the yellow anthers which clasp about the style at the front of the flower. The species grows in wet places, with hanging gardens being its principal habitat in Zion. Flowers are produced from late March to mid-May. Look for this plant at the Weeping Rock.

SPRING-BEAUTY
CLAYTONIA LANCEOLATA PURSH
PURSLANE FAMILY

This dainty rather fleshy perennial herb, with a solitary pair of opposite leaves, grows in moist places in the woods, along streams, and around springs. It blooms in springtime prior to leaves appearing on the oaks. The flowers are whitish to pink with darker pink veins. The small round underground stems or thickened roots can be eaten, either raw or cooked. The species is rather common in some of the moist places of the lower parts of the East Rim Trail.

WOODS ROSE
ROSA WOODSII LINDL.
ROSE FAMILY

"A rose by any other name would smell as sweet" and "a rose is a rose is a rose" apply as well to this species as to other roses. The large pink 5-petaled flowers on a spiny shrub with compound leaves are shared by no other plant in the Park. The fleshy swollen base of the flower contains numerous dry achenes intermixed with silvery hairs. Both the achenes, the dry true fruits, and the swollen flower base ripen, the latter to form the "rose fruit" or hip. The hips are slightly sour but can be eaten either raw or cooked, or made into wine, jam or jelly. The flowers, borne in summer, have been used in perfumes or as flavoring in syrup, and have even been candied.

This plant is also known as saltcedar. It has a gland on each leaf that secretes salt concentrated from water taken up by the roots. The salt falls back to the soil making it more salty and less attractive for plants other than tamarisk. The species was introduced from the Mediterranean region of the Old World during the early decades of this century and has spread by its windborne seeds over much of the West. The plant is called by some a ''well plant,'' because it pumps precious water from this arid land into the air. It forms dense thickets along streams in portions of the West and has been generally considered as an attractive nuisance. It flowers from spring to autumn.

ST. GEORGE MILKVETCH
ASTRAGALUS FLAVUS NUTT.
LEGUME FAMILY

Flowers vary from pinkish to white or even cream in this phase (var. *candicans* Gray) of a species with broad distribution and numerous variants. The plant is a spring flowering selenophyte, that is, it requires selenium for its life processes. Its presence in any particular place indicates that selenium is in the soil. The species is common on the Chinle Formation in the Park, and is especially abundant in the Petrified Forest sector. More that 150 different kinds of *Astragalus* are known to grow in Utah. It is a huge and complex genus with much variation.

BROAD-LEAVED LUPINE
LUPINUS LATIFOLIUS AGARDH.
LEGUME FAMILY

Lupines have palmately compound leaves and terminal racemes of brightly colored, but typically blue to purple, large flowers. Both annual and perennial species grow in Zion, the perennials mainly at higher elevations in the aspen and mountain brush communities. Broad-leaved lupine is a lower elevation species common in only Oak and Birch Creeks, where it grows on sandy terraces with cottonwood and oak. It is a widespread species in California, Oregon, and Washington, but its distribution in Zion is disjunct by more than two hundred miles from the nearest other population of the species. It is a beautiful species with its large flowers, which are borne in April and May.

LARKSPUR OR DELPHINIUM
DELPHINIUM ANDERSONII GRAY
BUTTERCUP FAMILY

There are three species of larkspur in the Park: the pale blue flowered scapose *Delphinium andersonii* var. *scaposum* (Greene) Welsh; the blue to blue purple *D. nuttallianum* Pritz or Nelson larkspur; and the dark purple to almost blackish *D. occidentale* (Wats.) Wats. var. *barbeyi* (Huth) Welsh or Barbey larkspur. The first two species flower in springtime, the last one in summer. The pale flowers of the scapose larkspur are produced in springtime in desert shrublands at low elevations in the Park. The others are middle to high elevation plants. They are separated easily by flower color and plant size. The Barbey larkspur typically is more than 3 feet tall; Nelson larkspur seldom more than a foot and a half. All are poisonous to livestock and potentially so to humans.

BLUELEAF ASTER
ASTER GLAUCODES BLAKE
SUNFLOWER FAMILY

This is the common aster of shady cutbanks along stream courses and roadways in much of the Park. The plant spreads by underground stems and forms patches. The bluish cast to the leaves and stems is due to a covering of wax, which prevents water loss. The plant blossoms in late summer and autumn. Ray flowers are white or less commonly tinged with pink. Zion's plants have glandular hairs on the flower heads and belong to var. *pulcher* (Blake) Kearney & Peebles.

SMOOTH PENSTEMON
PENSTEMON LAEVIS PENELL
FIGWORT FAMILY

Watch 'for this beautiful blue to lavender blue
flowered plant on the east side of the Park near
Checkerboard Mesa. The corollas have wine red
guidelines on the throat, providing a readily
visible target for visiting insects. Plants are
ordinarily 1 to 3 feet in height and are easily
seen. This is one of the parents of *Penstemon x
jonesii*, which was described earlier. The species
is well adapted to growth in sand or in crevices.
The Zion phase of the low penstemon or *Penstemon
humilis* Nutt. ex Gray var. *obtusifolius* (Pennell)
Reveal is a small plant (about a foot tall) of
crevices in sandstone over much of the Park. Look
for it in the Checkerboard Mesa region also. The
flowers, borne in springtime, are pale blue and
little more than half an inch long. It is known
only from Zion National Park and near vicinity.

BLUEDICKS
DICHELOSTEMMA PULCHELLUM (SALISB.) HELLER
LILY FAMILY

Growing amidst sagebrush, open woodlands, and coniferous forests in springtime, this blue lily has edible bulbs or corms, which are best eaten when roasted. Raw bulbs are objectionably mucilaginous. The flower clusters are called umbels (like a small umbrella) and indicate a relationship with onions, which are also edible. There is no odor or flavor of onion or garlic associated with bluedicks, however. The plants often grow up through shrubs, where they are protected from grazing animals such as the rock squirrel. The plants occur as individuals scattered through much of the lower elevation portions of the Park.

DORR OR DESERT SAGE
SALVIA DORRII (KELLOGG) ABRAMS
MINT FAMILY

This plant has a minty odor and flavor characteristic of members of the mint family. It is a silvery gray or whitish plant with opposite leaves and startlingly purple flowers borne in clusters from stem ends in springtime. Blossoms are produced in springtime where they contrast not only with the silvery gray of the foliage but with associated desert shrubs. Clays and silts as well as gravels serve as soils for this species. This is a relative of the common garden sage used to flavor meat and dressings. The seeds are reported to be edible, and the plant is said to have medicinal properites. Look for this plant along the slopes in Zion Canyon.

INDIGOBUSH
PSOROTHAMNUS FREMONTII (TORR.) BARNEBY
LEGUME FAMILY

Formerly placed in the genus *Dalea* (as *D. fremontii* Torr.), this plant is a thorny shrub with deep indigo flowers borne in clusters from stem ends during springtime. Branches that touch ground or rock open flowers first as they are warmed by sun when the air is still too cold to allow others to open. It is a desert shrub found only in the lower elevation parts of Zion. Watch for it in the Petrified Forest section of the Park. Indians have used the flowers, roots, and twigs, steeped in water, to make a yellow dye.

SPIDERWORT
TRADESCANTIA OCCIDENTALIS (BRITT) SMYTH
SPIDERWORT FAMILY

The word ending "wort" simply means herb or plant, or less commonly a root. Spider plant is probably no more a place for spider webs or residences than other plants, but they are occasionally so used. The sap is mucilaginous. Flower color varies from rose to pink, blue, or purple. The plants grow best in sandy sites, often where shaded by other plants, where they flower abundantly in early summer. They occur through much of the Park, but are especially common in Clear Creek Canyon east of the Tunnel.

HELLEBORINE
EPIPACTIS GIGANTEA DOUGL. EX HOOK
ORCHID FAMILY

Only a few orchids species occur in Zion, and usually the flowers are small and inconspicuous except for the entirety of the cluster. Helleborine is the exception to that rule. The flowers are large, up to an inch across, and they are moderately showy. The purple to purple brown of the flowers is easily seen on these plants of wet places along streams, seeps, and in some hanging gardens. Look for the dull flowers in springtime and early summer in wet vegetated places in the Zion Narrows.

WATER BIRCH
BETULA OCCIDENTALIS HOOK
BIRCH FAMILY

The Middle Fork of Taylor Creek in the Kolob District is a good place to see this water loving shrubby many stemmed tree. The bark is a dark reddish or purplish brown, smooth except for the conspicuous pale lenticels (corky spots). Male flowers are displayed in pendulous long catkins in early springtime before the leaves appear. Female catkins are shorter and more compact. They persist on the tree for a long time, finally breaking apart and releasing the tiny winged fruits that sail through the air like miniature aircraft. Various plant parts have been used medicinally.

MAIDENHAIR FERN
ADIANTUM CAPILLUS-VENERIS L.
COMMON FERN FAMILY

Two species of *Adiantum* occur in the Park, always in wet sites such as on the walls in hanging gardens. Both have leaflets with equally branched (dichotomous) venation and folded margins that obscure the spore bearing regions. That named above is the most common, occurring in all major wet sites in the Park. The second, the northern maidenhair or *Adiantum pedatum* L., is much less common and can be identified at a glance by its blackish leaf stalk that branches equally to form a symmetrically disposed blade of numerous leaflets. Both species turn yellow in autumn, dry to brown over winter, and grow fresh green leaves in springtime.

CANYON GRAPE
VITIS ARIZONICA ENGELM.
Grape Family

This native grape festoons oak, ash, and other trees and shrubs in Zion Canyon. It is the only native grape in Utah. The inconspicuous flowers are borne in springtime. Fruit is small and of poor flavor, but can be used to make jelly, jam, and wine of excellent flavor and quality. Leaves take on shades of red, orange, and other hues in autumn, adding to the exquisite beauty of the canyon bottom. The plant is especially prominent along the trail to Zion Narrows. In autumn the leaves turn color to subtle shades of red, orange, and yellow prior to falling and leaving the tangled mass of vine bare until springtime.

MORMON OR BRIGHAM TEA
EPHEDRA VIRIDIS COV.
EPHEDRA FAMILY

The round green stems of this plant appear similar to those of a scouring rush; both are photosynthetic and the leaves of both are reduced to mere scales or bracts. There the similarity ends, because Mormon or Brigham tea is a cone bearing, seed producing shrub. The male cones are borne on separate plants from the female cones. Dried twigs have been used to produce a tea by steeping them in hot water. The resulting tea is a pretty yellow orange in color and tastes not unlike water in which a stocking has been boiled. When flavored with sufficient sugar, mint, honey, or lemon, it makes a passable drink (so does plain hot water). Its local common names are derived from its early use by Mormons, approved by Brigham Young, as a substitute for coffee (which is forbidden).

UTAH JUNIPER
JUNIPERUS OSTEOSPERMA (TORR.) LITTLE
CYPRESS FAMILY

This is the other partner in the pinyon-juniper low forest in Zion National Park and widely in the Southwest. The juniper is the more drought tolerant of the pair and often serves as a nurse plant for the more water requiring pinyon pine, which grows up in the shade of the junipers. Wood is hard and has been used as a premier source of fence posts, called cedar posts, over much of the West. Cedar City, Cedar Breaks, and Cedar Mountain are named in reference to Utah juniper and its common name of cedar. The cones are fleshy and are called berries. Their flavor is poor, and they are seldom eaten by animals, but the large "pits" are drilled and used as beads by some Indians. The shreddy bark was used prehistorically by Indians for rough cordage, matting, and as diapers.

BIGTOOTH MAPLE
ACER GRANDIDENTATUM NUTT.
MAPLE FAMILY

The flowers of this plant, though cream to greenish, are really quite showy. They are produced in early springtime, as the leaves are expanding, and frequently go unnoticed by visitors to Zion. In autumn the leaves take on the brightest hues of red, maroon, orange, and other shades of any deciduous plant in the Park. The colors are made more intense by backgrounds of carbonaceous black stain on rock or dark red brown shades of weathered sandstone. A walk into the Zion Narrows in October is well worth the pain of icy water because of the brilliance of the maple display.

BOXELDER
ACER NEGUNDO L.
MAPLE FAMILY

Boxelder is a peculiar kind of maple with pinnately compound leaves of 3 to 5 leaflets, and with male flowers in drooping clusters and female flowers in racemes. Both male and female flowers are inconspicuous. The bark of twigs is green or suffused with red or red brown, and has a bitter sap. Boxelder bugs, marked black and red, feed on the leaves and give the plant another identifying feature. In springtime the sap has sugar in it, as in the sugar maple, and pioneers tapped the trees for its sweet juice, which was then concentrated to syrup by boiling. The trees grow along streams and rivers throughout Utah and much of the West. The leaves turn a disappointing yellow in autumn.

GAMBEL OAK
QUERCUS GAMBELII NUTT.
BEECH FAMILY

Also known as scrub oak, this clump forming plant occurs as low shrubs and exceptionally as moderate to large trees. The leaves have rounded lobes typical of the white oak group. Acorns are produced in abundance in some years, and were used as a source of food by Indians. They ripen in autumn and are rich in tannins and not of very good flavor. Reproduction is mainly by underground spreading stems, in spite of the tremendous number of seeds produced. Squirrels and other animals eat the seeds, which are also eaten by larvae of various insects. This plant forms hybrids with turbinella live-oak, which is evergreen; the hybrids are only partially evergreen and are most easily detected in winter when Gambel oak is without leaves. Wood is very hard and was used by Indians for digging sticks and for construction.

TURBINELLA LIVE-OAK
QUERCUS TURBINELLA GREENE
BEECH FAMILY

The leaves of turbinella live-oak resemble those of a holly plant. They are evergreen, leathery, and have prickly sharp lobes. The acorns are long, slender, and fall soon after maturity, with only the caps persisting on the branches. Wood is very tough and the many branched plants are essentially impenetrable. Tannin in the seeds must be removed prior to eating, which is usually done by grinding and soaking many changes of water until the tannin is removed, leaving a rather bland mush. Galls (swollen structures) on leaves were used medicinally as an astringent. The galls are caused by gall wasps, who lay their eggs on the plant. The plant accommodates the developing larvae by growing the gall home.

Along with Utah serviceberry this is the principal deciduous shrub of the pinyon-juniper community in Zion Canyon. It is anomalous (hence the scientific name) for an ash to have the leaves reduced to a single leaflet (rarely 3 or even 5 on some leaves), hence the common name. Fruits (samaras) are winged like one-half of a propeller and twirl to the ground when they break from the fruiting cluster (which is often more showy than the spring-borne flowers). This plant is especially notable along the road to the Kolob Canyon section of the Park.

VELVET ASH
FRAXINUS VELUTINA TORR.
Olive Family

This is a typical ash species with several leaflets in the compound leaves. It is a good sized deciduous tree of streamside and wetlands habitats in the bottom of Zion Canyon, where it grows with Fremont cottonwood and boxelder. It is often partially overgrown by canyon grape. The species reaches its natural northern limit nearby in Utah, but the plants are often cultivated as shade trees far north of Zion. The pollen has been cited as causing hay fever in susceptible persons in springtime. The wood is very tough and durable, but it is attacked by termites, sometimes while the tree is still alive.

PONDEROSA PINE
PINUS PONDEROSA LAWSON
PINE FAMILY

Also known as western yellow or bull pine, this is the common large pine tree of mesa tops and canyon rims in Zion. Individual trees appear as stick-like miniatures clinging to crevices in slickrock above the narrow gorge. Distance is deceiving, because, those trees that look so small from a distance might be 40 to 60 feet tall or more and 2 to 3 feet in diameter. The needles are mostly 3 to 4 inches long and are borne in clusters of three. The bark on old trees becomes divided into flattened cinnamon colored plates surrounded by deep dark cracks. The wood is considered as a first rate construction lumber, and the trees in much of Zion were cut for timber prior to establishment of the Park. Birds and squirrels eat the seeds, which are generally considered as too small for human food.

FREMONT COTTONWOOD
POPULUS FREMONTII WATS.
WILLOW FAMILY

This plant is well named both commonly and scientifically. The mature capsules of female trees release hair tufted (the cotton) seeds, which sometimes clothe the ground and other plants and collect on pools of water as a cottony mass. The scientific name commemorates John Charles Fremont, pathfinder, botanical explorer, presidential candidate, and soldier, who camped beneath its shade on numerous occasions during his exploration of the West. The broad leaves are similar to aspen, to which it is related, but the shape of the tree and its habitat are remarkably different. In much of the Southwest, this is the only broadleaved tree of waterways, providing for the traveler cooling shade and the possibility of water.

ASPEN
POPULUS TREMULOIDES MICHX.
WILLOW FAMILY

This pretty white barked tree of high mountain slopes and summits is also known as quaking aspen or quakey. These latter names are derived from the trembling quality of the leaves; they move even in the most gentle breeze. The ability to quake is due to the flattened leaf stalks, which give strength to the stalk in an up-down direction but are weak in side to side direction. Catkins are produced in springtime. The wood is used for firewood, match sticks, and to line saunas. Fence posts made from aspen last for such a short time that they are seldom used for that purpose. Inner bark of this and others of the genera *Populus* and *Salix* have the substances salicin and populin, aspirin precursors. They were used by Indians, explorers, and pioneers as aspirin is today.

SILK-TASSEL BUSH
GARRYA FLAVESCENS WATS.
SILK-TASSEL FAMILY

The smooth brown bark of this evergreen shrub causes it to be mistaken sometimes for a manzanita. The leaves are dull, however, and bluish rather than shiny, and the flowers are borne in drooping tassels that give the bush its common name. Flowers are produced very early, in some seasons as early as January but more commonly in February or March. The flavor of the plant is bad. One taste will convince a person never to try it again. The leaves contain Garryine, a poisonous alkaloid, used in medicine. The plant can be seen along the trail to Emerald Pools.

NEEDLE AND THREAD GRASS
STIPA COMATA TRIN. & RUPR.
GRASS FAMILY

There are a great many grasses in Zion National Park. Perhaps the most distinctive of the dryland types is needle and thread grass, with its long needle and thread-like awns that twist upon drying. The awn base is flattened and takes up water from rain or dew and uncoils, only to coil again when water evaporates. The tail of the awn catches in other vegetation and the coiling and uncoiling of the awn serves to drive the sharp tip of the floret into the earth or into other plants. This action is an aid in planting this beautiful species, which can be seen in springtime along the slopes bordering the Watchman Trail.

JONES REEDGRASS
CALAMAGROSTIS SCOPULORUM JONES
GRASS FAMILY

This clumpforming grass with drooping leaves is characteristic of the hanging gardens in Zion National Park. Its distribution in the gardens is separate from a wider dispersal in mountainous areas from Montana south to Arizona and New Mexico. The species was named from specimens taken near Springdale by pioneer botanist Marcus E. Jones, who first visited Zion Canyon in 1894. Watch for this plant in the hanging gardens along the Narrows Trail, where it flowers in late summer and autumn.

Balsamroot, Arrowleaf
Birch, Water
Bitterbrush
Blackbrush
Bluedicks
Bottlebrush
Buffaloberry, Roundleaf
Camissonia, Yellow
Claretcup
Cliffrose
Clover, Lean
Cryptanth, Golden
Daisy, Canaan
Daisy, Utah
Daisy, Zion
Draba, Zion
Encelia, Bush
Evening-primrose, Pale
Evening-primrose, Tufted
Filaree
Four O'Clock, Large
Gilia, Nuttall
Gilia, Scarlet
Globemallow
Goldenaster
Grounsel, Uinta
Helleborine
Indigobush
Larkspur
Lily, Sego
Locus, New Mexico
Lupine, Broad-leaved
Mahogony, Mountain
Mahonia, Creeping
Mahonia, Fremont
Manzanita, Mexican
Marigold, Desert
Milkvetch, St. George

Milkvetch, Stinking
Milkvetch, Zion
Milkweed, Spider
Monkeyflower, Cardinal
Paintbrush, Common
Paintbrush, Slickrock
Penstemon, Eaton
Penstemon, Jones
Penstemon, Palmer
Penstemon, Smooth
Penstemon, Utah
Phlox, Desert
Pricklypear, Plains
Prince's Plume
Purple Torch
Rockcress, Common
Sage, Desert
Saltbush, Fourwing
Sand-verbena, Fragrant
Seepwillow, Emory
Serviceberry, Utah
Shooting Star, Zion
Skunkbush
Snowberry, Mountain
Solomon-seal, False
Springbeauty
Stoneseed, Showy
Sweetpea, Zion
Tamarisk
Thistle, Arizona
Thistle, New Mexico
Trefoil
Wallflower, Western
Wedgeleaf
Weed, Butterfly
Weed, Rattlesnake
Yucca, Datil
Yucca, Utah

SUMMER

Angels-trumpet
Aster, Blueleaf
Bottlebrush
Cholla, Whipple
Columbine, Golden
Columbine, Western
Daisy, Zion
Elderberry, Blue
Encelia, Bush
Eriogonum, Thompson
Evening-primrose, Pale
Evening-primrose, Tufted
Flax, Blue
Four O'Clock, Large
Gilia, Scarlet
Groundsel, Broom
Ivy, Poison
Lobelia, Scarlet
Madder
Monkeyflower, Cardinal
Penstemon, Jones
Penstemon, Palmer
Prickly Poppy
Rose, Wood
Sagebrush, Sand
Sand-verbena, Fragrant
Seepwillow, Emory
Snowberry, Mountain
Spiderwort
Stoneseed, Showy
Tamarisk
Watercress
Weed, Butterfly

FALL

Angels-trumpet
Aster, Blueleaf
Bottlebrush
Camissonia, Yellow
Eriogonum, Thompson
Flower, Hummmingbird
Four O'Clock, Large
Gilia, Scarlet
Globemallow
Groundsel, Broom
Lobelia, Scarlet
Madder
Prickly Poppy
Rabbitbrush, Rubber
Sage, Big
Sagebrush, Sand
Sand-verbena, Fragrant
Seepwillow, Emory
Snakeweed, Broom
Spiraea, Rock
Tamarisk

INDEX

INDEX

THE AUTHOR

Dr. Stanley L. Welsh has been collecting plants in Utah since 1953. After completing his Master of Science degree at Brigham Young University, he received his PhD at Iowa State University in 1960.

Dr. Welsh has collected plants extensively throughout the Great Plains, from Canada to the Texas Panhandle. He has collected in all the counties of Utah and the neighboring states of Idaho, Nevada, Wyoming, Colorado, New Mexico, and Arizona. The herbarium at Brigham Young University which Dr. Welsh oversees includes collections from all of the United States. He has also done considerable work in western Canada and Alaska.

Dr. Welsh has written numerous scientific papers on the plants of the Colorado Plateau areas and has published many papers on the flora of the national parks and monuments in Utah. Some of his papers have focused on the state's endangered plant species. Presently Dr. Welsh is the Director of the Monte L. Bean Museum at Brigham Young University, where he continues to teach botany and plant classification. He is known internationally as a plant taxonomist for species in western North America. Stanley Welsh has been a good friend of the national parks in Utah for many years, contributing generously of his time to further their preservation.